# Poodling

1263

*(preceding pages)*
01
A POODLING POTPOURI:
MICROPHONES, BALLS,
& OTHER VEGETAL
DEFORMATIONS.
BERKELEY, CALIFORNIA.

02
*(on the right)*
INGROWN POODLING:
DENSITY AT THE BORDER
OF TOPIARY—AND YET
INDIVIDUALLY SHAPED.
EL CERRITO, CALIFORNIA.

MARSHMALLOW CLUMPS.
SCOTTSDALE, ARIZONA.

# Poodling:

## On the Just Shaping of Shrubbery

Marc Treib

*Photos by the author*
*(unless otherwise noted)*

ORO EDITIONS, NOVATO, CALIFORNIA

Book Design: Marc Treib
ORO Project Coordinator: Jake Anderson

First Edition
Library of Congress data available upon request.
ISBN: 978-1-957183-82-4
International Distribution: www.oroeditions.com/distribution
10 9 8 7 6 5 4 3 2 1
First edition
World Rights: Available

Color Separations and Printing: ORO Group Ltd.
Printed in China

For Chip Sullivan

and

Elizabeth Boults

03
HEDGEROWS.
CANTERBURY PLAIN,
NEW ZEALAND.

04
CLASSIC PIN CUSHION
—OR BALL—POODLING.
PALM SPRINGS, CALIFORNIA.

It is well known among landscape historians that in the ancient Roman world the gardener was known by the Latin title *topiarius*, a figure often depicted holding an ax rather than a trowel or a spade. The ax signified maintenance—and one might add, control—a triumph of human intervention over natural processes. But why reconfigure the branches of a tree or shrub? Why not just leave them to grow as directed by their genetics and responses to the environment? Horticultural practices such as grafting and pruning improve the health of the plant and increase its yield; but shaping serves other purposes as well. Densely planted rows of trees confront the force of the wind while rendering property lines visible. At smaller scale hedges perform similar duties. Like good fences, good hedges can make good neighbors. To improve their visual aspects, and at times to address civic propriety, domestic hedges are commonly sheared into a more ordered form, unlike hedgerows, which are usually left to grow without undue trimming.[1] On New Zealand's Canterbury Plain, however, hedgerows are clipped into neat volumes with the precision and pride normally associated with the English lawn [03]. These masses of vegetation, unlike most hedgerows, are transformed into colossal works of topiary art high and long. Whether at the smaller domestic scale, or with the greater dimensions demanded by terrain and climate, responses to functional constraints such as these may have been the origins of topiary as an artistic practice. First need, then art [04].

In the garden, however, other forces are operative. Once the shrub had been considered as a material for sculpting, it was only a small step before someone realized that a living hedge could be treated as an architectural feature such as a wall, or a freestanding shrub as material for a work of art. Considering the training and shearing of living vegetation as acts of artistic creation, the fantasy of those with shears took hold. Clouds have been read as animals; the surface of the moon interpreted as a human face or a rabbit; and stars of constellations imagined as human and animal figures. Why then could one not see in the shrub the possibilities for architectonic and figurative forms? Although decried by some as a perverse tic—as do certain nature purists—that perversity has driven invention as a source of novelty. At times sheared vegetation provokes a smile on the face of the viewer; at times it even creates a *frisson* of shear delight. A shrub metamorphosed into a fish? A tea cup [05, 06]? A bird? A lion? Adam and Eve? Ah, the mind may run rampant. And it has.

Though the practice probably began centuries before, in Roman times Pliny the Younger (CE 62–110) told of the widespread practice of shaping shrubs, and listed the variety of its manifestations. In speaking of the gardens of ex-urban Roman villas he noted that: "box is cut into a thousand different forms: some into letters expressing the name of the master; sometimes that of the artificer's, whilst here and there little obelisks rise, intermixed with fruit trees." Pliny said it in Latin, of course, but you get the idea. Already in Roman times topiary took both figurative and geometric forms, boxwood and cypress being the species most commonly used.[2] In more recent years, additional species have joined them as agreeable alternatives, among them Monterey cypress (*Cupressus macrocarpa*), pyracantha (*Arbutus laurocerasus*), laurel (*Laurus nobilus*), juniper (*Juniperus* spp.), and English yew (*Taxus baccata*). Although other species have been figuratively pruned, the resulting efforts have not always proved to be successful. The size and density of the needles or leaves affect the shaping, as does the plant's rate of growth. The shrub, almost stubbornly, does not always exactly respond to the lofty intentions of the *topiarius*.

Topiary confounds human expectations by transforming a plant into a non-natural shape, at times zoomorphic, but more often geometric. In the process, the unruly product of natural growth is tamed, controlled, and modeled into a form that expresses some human desire. As noted above, pruning is at root horticulturally beneficial by increasing the heartiness and/or yield of the fruit tree. Espaliering collects increased sunlight along the length of its branches, thus augmenting growth and ultimately the plant's bounty [07, 08]. Although in English we adopted the verb and noun espalier from the French, the practice is said to have originated in Italy some time in the late sixteenth century (the French *espalier* deriving from the Italian *spalliera*).[3] Appearing almost deflated in their reduced depth, the plants—most often fruits—have been compressed into a single plane supported by a trellis, wires, or mounted against a wall. Within some sheltered gardens the wall has been dispensed with and the

05
FISH(ES) TOPIARY.
LOS ANGELES,
CALIFORNIA.

06
TEAPOT TOPIARY.
LUHACOVICE,
SLOVAKIA.

*(following pages)*
07 *(above)*
ESPALIERS OF
DIFFERENT SPECIES.
LOS ANGELES,
CALIFORNIA.

08 *(below)*
ESPALIERS IN TIERS.
FOREST LAWN
CEMETERY,
GLENDALE, CALIFORNIA.

plants coerced to grow on fences or on wires strung between posts. The benefits from these practices include eased maintenance and harvesting. In less temperate climates, the plants also profit from the heat retained in the thermal mass of the supporting wall. To trap the heat from sunlight, and further thwart the effects of frost, glass panels enclose the support structure during the colder months. Perhaps the most extensive examples of this prosthetic device are found fronting the retaining walls of the terraces on the great Sanssouci estate in Potsdam, Germany [9, 10]. In Italy, a related practice was the seasonal installation of glass walls and roofs on the *limonaia* structures found near Verona, along the shores of Lago de Garda, that are used to retain the heat of sunlight to ensure a providential crop.

Le Potager de Roi, the kitchen garden of Louis XIV's Versailles, is perhaps the most exquisite representative of espaliering, a protected zone filled with fences and walls rich with low-hanging fruit, numerous types of pears among them [11]. Under the direction of Jean-Baptiste de la Quintinie the garden was constructed from 1678–83. Its fruit production continues even today, more than three centuries after its creation, and the garden serves as a ready reference for those studying landscape architecture and horticulture at the school that occupies buildings adjacent to it.[4] The garden's carefully groomed products, I am told, are sold in some of the more upscale produce shops in Paris, thus still serving an aristocracy, in this case one based on wealth rather than bllodline alone.

Remaining at Versailles, let us return to topiary per se: topiary in the main gardens of the grand domain that lies not far from the Potager. The use of flowers and planted beds known as *parterre de broiderie* ("embroidery on the ground") was a staple of the French formal garden of the long seventeenth century, the era of autocracy, the era of Louis XIV [12]. Boxwood (*Buxus sempervirens*) was commonly used to outline beds then planted with flowers, gravel, or filled with water, and its use ran rampant in the gardens of the Sun King.[5] These lines of box tended to be clipped low, rarely more than a foot in height, and read as bands rather than volumes. When the boxwood is allowed to grow taller, like other species it is shaped into geometric forms, often a kind of attenuated cone with aspirations to be an obelisk [13]. Here topiary serves as inter-

9, 10
SCHLOSS SANSOUCI.
POTSDAM, GERMANY, 1746.
GLASS PANELS ARE CLOSED SEASONALLY TO RETAIN THE HEAT OF THE SUN.

*(following pages)*
11
JEAN-BAPTISTE DE LA QUINTINIE.
POTAGER DU ROI.
VERSAILLES, FRANCE, 1660s.

12, 13
ANDRÉ LE NÔTRE.
ORANGERIE.
VERSAILLES, FRANCE,
1663–1693.
ORDER IN THE PLAN;
ORDER IN THE PLANTS.

mediary or ambassador between architecture and garden, between construction and vegetation. A certain tension haunts the practice of topiary. Despite the purity, and often beauty, of its forms—especially shortly after pruning—one senses the plant's seeking to free itself from the confinement of its sheared form, ever trying to regain what should be its proper shape. Perhaps this is the reason why in 1995 a non-profit organization dedicated to "promoting better pruning and gardening" held a contest for "Bizarre Yard Art," and issued a post card picturing its four winners—two of which would qualify as quite inventive topiary.[6]

In England a century or so after Versailles, garden makers did not hold such a fond opinion of this manner of vegetal management. In the *Spectator*, Joseph Addison (1672–1719) voiced his criticism that:

> *Our Trees rise in Cones, Globes, and Pyramids. We see the Marks of the Scissors upon every Plant and Bush. I do not know whether I am singular in my Opinion, but, for my own part, I would rather look upon a Tree in all its Luxuriance and Diffusion of Boughs and Branches, than when it is thus cut and trimmed into a Mathematical Figure.*[7]

He was not alone in his preferences. Alexander Pope joined the battle in his celebrated "Epistle to Lord Burlington" (1731), condemning the symmetry and rigidity of past eras and the criminal acts that formal garden makers had inflicted upon the land and its vegetation:

> *Grove nods to Grove, each Ally has a Brother,*
> *And half the Platform just reflects the other.*
> *The suff'ring Eye inverts Nature sees,*
> *Trees cut to Statues, Statues thick as Trees.*[8]

Perhaps neither Addison nor Pope had experienced the grandeur of allées of mature beeches at Versailles, or the beautiful flanks of trees that line European roads; while far from naturalistic in alignment, these trees nonetheless display great "Luxuriance and Diffusion of Boughs and Branches" [14, 15]. Pope was hardly the only English voice to condemn formality in the garden's planning—or the trimming of its vegetation. Over a decade earlier, an anonymous author

had written disparaging:

*Trees clipt to Statues, monsters, cats and dogs,*
*And hillies metamorphos'd into hogs;*
*Here urns and statues in confusion stand,*
*And one wide waste of riches spread the land.*

Harsh. Versailles, and its courtiers, receive similar condemnation:

*Trifles like those at proud Versailles combin'd,*
*Fools to surprise, and shock the tasteful mind.*[9]

Tsk, tsk. As if there were only one all-mighty taste that one must accept as governing such matters. "Not hardly," as my friends in the South might say.

Although the argument is usually stated in aesthetic terms as the opposition of formal against naturalistic design, other reasons contributed to the shift in the preference for unclipped plants, among them the resentment to autocracies such as those of the French Grand Siècle. In this brand of thought neither geometry nor the shears, but Nature itself should serve as the source for the garden and park. Even the perception of cultivated land could be deemed beautiful if properly framed and amended. Addison suggested that small gestures could have great effect, for example that a field of corn can "make a pleasant Prospect, and if the Walks were a little taken care of that lie between them." In addition, "if the natural Embroidery of the Meadows were helpt and improved by some small Additions of Art," he offered, "and the several Rows of Hedges set off by Trees and Flowers, that the Soil was capable of receiving, a Man might make a pretty Landskip of his Possessions."[10] Note that "Rows of Hedges"—perhaps some of them sheared—and "Additions of Art" were still mandatory. That is to say, it was from the combination of the "made" and the natural that a "pretty Landskip" resulted.

A century had passed since the rise of the English Landscape Garden when author and humorist Mark Twain expressed a regained appreciation for the formal garden, despite the burden of rigorous maintenance and the politics of its origins. In *Innocents Abroad, or the New Pilgrims' Progress*, published in 1869, Twain tells of his encounter with the gardens of Versailles as he and a group of pilgrims passed through Europe on one leg of their extended journey to the Holy Land. Clearly the American

14
WILLIAM KENT.
ROUSHAM.
OXFORDSHIRE,
ENGLAND, 1732.

15
ANDRÉ LE NÔTRE.
A GRAND ALLÉE
IN THE PARK.
VERSAILLES, FRANCE,
1663–1693.

author was impressed and nearly overwhelmed by his experience of what Louis XIV hath wrought—with some help from André le Nôtre and thousands of workers, to be sure. "You gaze, you stare, and try to understand that it is real, that it is on the earth, that it is not the Garden of Eden—but your brain grows giddy, stupefied by the world of beauty around you, and you half believe you are the dupe of an exquisite dream."[11] His description of the vast garden of the Sun King continues with a detailed description of the richness of the garden's features and the extent of its dimensions. Like those more naturally inclined today, Twain, "always thought ill of people at home, who trimmed their shrubbery into pyramids and squares and spires and all of unnatural shapes," who "distort a dozen sickly trees into unaccustomed shapes in a little yard no bigger than a dining-room." In that context, he admits, they "surely look absurd."[12] But when he encountered this very same practice and its products at Versailles, a light was revealed unto him—and he was stunned. It was not a question of trimming and shaping alone, but the volume, the extent, the number, and the precision of the forms—all the products of the ax and the shears as well as the mind. "The trees in no two avenues are shaped alike," he notes, the result being that, "the eye is not fatigued with anything in the nature of mathematical uniformity."[13] Variety is the spice of garden experience as well as life, and here in the grand domain of Versailles variety was found in the "fifty different shapes" that produce "quaint effects [that] are infinitely picturesque" [16].[14] Unlike St. Paul whose conversion, it is said, resulted from his falling from a horse, Twain's conversion stemmed (pun intended) from his encounter with beautifully managed and composed greenery, where management had raised gardening and the garden to an art.

In the later nineteenth century, closing in on the arrival of the twentieth, topiary was once again decried by those who sought a more appropriate expression for nature in the garden: by proposing nature *as* the garden. A leading figure in this movement was the Irish gardener and author William Robinson in books such as *The Wild Garden* (1870) and *The English Flower Garden* (1893). In the *Wild Garden*, Robinson devotes most of his writing to the presentation of interesting, beautiful, and suitable plants and perhaps their pairing, but otherwise offers little discussion of the greater order that the garden should assume [17]. He decries the inordinate pruning he has witnessed as common practice in the maintenance of London's parks. "The mere fact of men having to pass through one of those shrubberies every autumn, and, as they fancy, 'prune' and otherwise attend to the unfortunate shrubs and low trees," he writes,

> *leads to... the shrubs taking the appearance of inverted besoms. ...Any interesting life that might be in the ground is destroyed, and the whole appearance of the shrubbery is made hideous from the point of view of art; all good culture of flowering or evergreen shrubs destroyed or made impossible.*[15]

It seems that to Robinson art is to be found only in the selection of the garden's plants, rather than in a design in which human intervention is apparent. He suggests that one achieves art by planting a potentially beautiful species—always with regard to the plants adjacent and around it—tends it, and then contentedly witnesses its flowering and aesthetic effect. How all those plants amalgamate into a total work of art is left unmentioned, implying that the garden coheres as a collection of these individual acts.[16]

For every argument there is always a counter-argument, whether as an expression of the Asian philosophical concept of *yin/yang*, or the Hegelian idea of the thesis and opposing antithesis eventually—at least hopefully—combining to form a new synthesis. That desired synthesis was found in the landscapes of Gertrude Jekyll, where a wild or wooded garden usually accompanies the more rigorous lines of herbaceous borders marked by a brilliant play of textures and colors [18]. Jekyll's fruitful collaborations with architect Edwin Lutyens produced stunning gardens that intertwined the formality of a highly architectonic structure with the informality of the plantings—for example, in the Great Plat that occupies the center of the Hestercombe garden in Taunton (1907) [19]. Here the rigor of Lutyens's geometry is dampened, enriched, and enlivened by Jekyll's artistic composition of the plants according to hue, mass, texture, and times of bloom. Only very rarely, however, were the shrubs in a Jekyll garden sheared into fanciful shapes. Like Robinson, she greatly appreciated the inherent qualities of each species and used them to great effect in her lushly planted gardens.

Like all that is fashionable, the trend for confining shrubbery in geometric or fanciful forms has come and gone like the phases of the moon, whether by the dictates of contemporary taste, a lack of interest, or an insufficient purse for maintenance. Certainly,

16
ANDRÉ LE NÔTRE.
WATER AVENUE.
VERSAILLES, FRANCE,
1660s+.
ALTERNATION OF THE CAST
AND THE PRUNED.

17
ALFRED PARSONS.
'COLONIES OF POET'S
NARCISSUS AND BROAD-
LEAVED SAXIFRAGE."
[WILLIAM ROBINSON,
*THE WILD GARDEN*]

18
GERTRUDE JEKYLL.
MUNSTEAD WOOD.
GUILFORD, ENGLAND,
1897.
THE WOODLAND.

19
GERTRUDE JEKYLL.
HESTERCOMBE.
TAUNTON, ENGLAND,
1907.
GREAT PLAT.

as the economy of large estates waned in post-WW1 Britain, and the number of their gardeners was highly reduced, the aesthetic call for maintaining topiary in tight forms was relaxed. In some gardens topiary even disappeared completely. The primary exceptions were found in the gardens of those with means, or those who upheld the banner for maintaining heritage as found in traditional forms. We can be very happy that certain great works of topiary have endured, or have been resurrected in a state true to their origins [20, 21].[17] Located in Cumbria, Levens Hall must be the grandest of the surviving topiary circuses. Its greenery mixes the fanciful with the geometric, all accompanied by curious hybrids, several of which appear as giant green mushrooms. This topiary garden is said to have been created by the gardener Guillaume Beaumont between the years 1689 and 1712, although one wonders how much of what delights us today had reached maturity during the Beaumont years. Even under favorable conditions, plants require time and care to mature and to respond to the pruning inflicted upon them.[17] In his own garden of Great Dixter in Surrey, Christopher Lloyd maintained a topiary and lawn garden planted by his father in the late nineteenth century. At Nymans, also in Surrey, created by Ludwig Meissel around 1890, exist some wonderful examples of the gardener's art [22]. These include whimsical objects in the guise of chess pieces, tea pots, or other forms that suggest—but do not precisely announce—any specific reference. Unlike the poodled shrub, which expresses the character of its branches individually, in topiary forms it is the whole rather than the part which prevails as the subject of the work.

While perhaps no collection of topiary can match the longevity, variety, and grandeur of Levens Hall, two gardens in the United States appear to have taken up the challenge and produced landscapes almost exclusively displaying creating topiary in its various guises: as hedge, architecture, and figure.

20 *(previous pages)*
21 *(opposite above)*
GUILLAUME BEAUMONT.
LEVENS HALL.
CUMBRIA, ENGLAND,
1689–1712,
A WONDERLAND OF
VEGETAL FORMS.

22 *(opposite below)*
TOPIARY FORM.
LUDWIG MEISSEL ET AL.
NYMANS GARDEN.
HANDCROSS, SUSSEX,
ENGLAND.

*(following pages)*
23, 24
LADEW TOPIARY GARDEN.
MONKTON, MARYLAND,
BEGUN 1920S.
A VERITABLE VEGETAL
MENAGERIE.

25, 26
JOSEPH CARREIRO;
GEORGES MENDONCA.
GREEN ANIMALS.
PORTSMOUTH,
RHODE ISLAND, 1905+.
POULTRY, PYRAMIDS
& SWAGS IN GREENERY.

Ladew Topiary Garden in Monkton, Maryland—with origins in the 1920s—is bounded by a massive, neatly trimmed hedge into which attractive swags have been cut and modeled: the hedge as architecture [23]. In one area of the lawn, a horse and rider hurdle a low hedge as if members of a steeplechase; before them run a pack of rapacious topiary hounds, no doubt in pursuit of an elusive fox. The horse and rider may also refer to Pimlico Race Course in nearby Baltimore. In another area of the garden, the vista opens to a field of the more architectural topiary forms that populate the length of the green promenade that traces the contour of the land [24].

Green Animals in Portsmouth, Rhode Island, is more intimate in feeling and fanciful throughout [25, 26]. The garden and its menagerie are the creation of two gardeners: the Portuguese-born Joseph Carreiro, who tended the garden from 1905 until his death in 1945, and Georges Mendonca, who succeeded his father-in-law and maintained the garden's original high standard until his own retirement in 1985.[18] The garden lays claim to more than eighty pieces of individual topiary that as a group conjure a green wonderland worthy of a visit by Alice. Among the inhabitants of this vegetal zoo are a giraffe, donkey, bear, both a momma and baby duck, elephant, dog—and for some unknown reason, a policeman. Accompanying them are the more common green garden forms such as a chair, a lantern, and a spiraling pyramid or two.

It takes time, patience, and thus money, to produce topiary forms, and various methods have been used to achieve the desired forms within a shorter period of time or with less expenditure. And one must admit that seen shortly after pruning and reshaping have taken place, the joyous effect produced by topiary in full leaf may evaporate in a tangle of exposed branches. But give it time: the new growth will again come to blanket the structure, complete the form, and generate the amusement intended by its maker. Historically topiary was fashioned purely from the shrub, and guided and shaped into the desired form as it grew. The desired profile was then maintained by periodic shearing. Employing this technique years might pass before an identifiable figure or form emerged from the shrubbery. To speed the process, vines or other suitable plants have been draped within or upon a framework of some type. The noted British landscape theorist J. C. Loudon understood the need for shortcuts, and early in the nineteenth century suggested that: "Vegetable sculptures are very appropriate in parterres and other scenes in the ancient style. That they may be executed with correctness and without loss of time, the skeleton can be formed of wire."[19] Today chicken wire or other metal mesh might be used, especially should the landscape artist wish to sculpt images not easily achieved with shrubs that grow from their roots up, at their own pace, and whose branch structure must be accommodated. Fanciful figures such as the Muppets enacted in vegetation; or an astronaut descending to a green lunar surface—or even a vegetal reenactment in three-dimensions of Georges Seurat's pointillist painting *Sunday Afternoon on Grand Jatte*, have all been achieved by growing plants over a frame [27, 28, 29, 30]. In the case of the latter, at least at the time of my visit some years ago, the frame was visible in places where the vegetal cover had retreated, thereby revealing the prosthetic structure needed to initiate and maintain the configurations of the green figures. The Belgian landscape architect Erik Dhont uses metal frameworks of substantial dimensions to guide the development of the shaped blocks of hedges that will serve as the garden's primary visual features, blocks that also define and articulate the spaces within. One of his recent gardens in Belgium—seen here in an early state—provides an excellent illustration of how the processes of growth and pruning utilize support structures to achieve the designer's intended form [31].

By devoting attention to the practice of topiary—whether in figure, form, or hedge—my intention is to provide neither a complete history nor catalog of all its major examples; after all, the practice is world-wide and a number of books have already been written on the subject. Instead my reason for first introducing topiary is to provide the historical background for the shaping of shrubbery and trees, and to illustrate some of the gardener's attempts at absolute control. In topiary, the plant is forced to assume a singular form with its growth held in check. This approach differs considerably from the practice of poodling, where a negotiation—a give and take—occurs between the gardener and the shrub. In many instances, I would guess that the intention to poodle came long after the shrub had grown, perhaps due to a gardener's whim, perhaps because the plant was not growing in as a perfect a form as desired, or that a true topiary form was unachievable. This would suggest that one basis for turning to

27
ASTRONAUT TOPIARY.
MELBOURNE, FLORIDA,
1980s.

28
MUPPETS TOPIARY.
BATH, ENGLAND, 1970s.

29, 30 *(opposite below)*
JAMES T. MASON.
*A SUNDAY AFTERNOON ON GRAND JATTE.*
COLUMBUS, OHIO,
c. 2000.
GEORGES SEURAT'S CELEBRATED PAINTING ENACTED IN GREENERY OVER A METAL FRAME.

31
ERIK DHONT.
GARDEN IN BELGIUM,
2005+.
FRAMEWORKS TO GUIDE THE GROWTH AND SHAPING OF THE SHRUBS.

poodling is expressed in the old adage: "If you can't beat 'em, join 'em"—or in this case, "clip 'em."

Topiary is neither a gardening practice restricted to the past, nor the sole province of the New World or central Europe. It has also been found in Asia, and probably Africa as well. Japan has provided us with examples that demonstrate strong parallels in the clipping of shrubs, and may have actually fostered the origins of a pruning manner we now term poodling.

## Origins in Japan?

Japanese gardeners have rarely displayed any reticence in bringing plants and nature under their control, limited only by the country's cultural norms and the available technology [32]. Agriculture is by nature an artificial practice that intervenes in what might be considered true natural processes. In a nation in which historically less than ten percent of its territory was arable, the need for increasing production was accomplished by augmenting the amount of productive terrain by terracing and reclamation. The enrichment of the soil below ground supported the plants propagated on its surface. Rice fields were seasonally flooded, with seedings thereafter inserted in neat rows to promote even growth and facilitate their harvest. In all probability pruning also responded to agronomic need. If the ground itself was open to modification, why not the forms of the plants that were nurtured by it?[20]

Trees were also pruned for reasons less horticultural and more aesthetic. Historically, Japanese architectonic space was considered to be a primarily horizontal phenomenon, a continuity defined and shaped by buildings, trees, and shrubs. This preference for horizontality, and for buildings suitably related to the ground plane, shaped arboricultural practices as well. These efforts to "horizontalize" tree canopies endure even today [33]. Clipping intermediate tree branches, and thinning leaf and pine needle clusters, interject carefully considered horizontal voids into tree canopies consequently transformed into stacks of dense green layers. The enormous amount of labor exerted in shaping these trees for artistic reasons produced corresponding botanical consequences, not all of them positive. For example, pruning into distinct horizontal units can seriously reduce the ability of the branches to resist

32
JIKO-IN.
NARA, JAPAN,
17TH CENTURY.
PRUNING INTO LAYERS.

33
KINKAKU-JI.
KYOTO, JAPAN,
14TH; 20TH CENTURY.
THE COLLECTIVE EFFECT OF SHAPING TREE CANOPIES INTO HORIZONTAL LAYERS.

the weight of dead loads placed upon them. In extreme situations, snowfall collected upon the clumps of needles remaining after pruning can snap even large branches. Understanding the hazard, gardeners seasonally reinforce these branches with straw ropes suspended from a central pole. Like so many other traditional gardening techniques the installation of these winter supports is still used today, and in the garden of Kenroku-en in Kanazawa one finds the most beautiful examples of these seasonal structural reinforcements [34].

As in the West, pruning first served horticultural purposes. Tea plants (*Camellia sinensis*) are commonly grown in rows, whether on flat land or hillsides, in climates suitably cool and suitably moist. To yield a product more rich and flavorful, the leaves are plucked while still young, a practice that also stimulates continued new growth. The process of harvesting juvenile foliage has led to plants eternally constrained into almost Platonic forms. Their beauty lies not only in the individual shrub, but also collectively in rows that run the length of hillside terraces, or trace the contours of the terrain. Not only in Asia, but even on islands in the middle of the Atlantic Ocean [35].

Lore has it that early Japanese tea masters like Takeno Jō-ō (1502–55) and Sen-no-Rikyu (1522–1591) saw the aesthetic potential of using sheared shrubs in the tea garden—perhaps bringing with them thoughts of the beverage's origin. Thereafter, plants were routinely shaped to enrich a garden's composition and heighten its beauty. Once again, what had begun as a functional technique was adapted and used purely for its visual appeal. Over the years Japanese temple gardens came to combine noticeably clipped shrubs with those allowed to maintain their more natural guise. At the garden of Shōden-ji in northern Kyoto sheared azaleas serve as surrogates for the stones more commonly used in dry (*karesansui*) gardens [36]. Although essentially topiary in their unitary forms, being vegetal they stand apart from the white walls that enclose them and the naturalism found in the trees and other vegetation beyond the wall.

34
KENROKU-EN.
KANAZAWA, JAPAN,
17TH CENTURY+.
IN WINTER, STRAW ROPES SUSPENDED FROM A CENTRAL POLE COUNTER THE WEIGHT OF THE SNOW ON BRANCHES WEAKENED BY PRUNING.

Shōden-ji embodies the Japanese aesthetic concept of *shin-gyō-sō*, which might be loosely translated as the mixture of formal, semiformal, and informal elements. The categorization of differing degree of formalities had its origins in calligraphy. *Shin* is the formal mode: possibly stiff,

clear, and easily legible; read ideograph by ideograph, as if letter by letter. Applied to Western letter forms *shin* might qualify the elegant Roman capitals used for inscriptions on public monuments and governmental buildings. *Sō*, at the opposite end of the scale, relates to cursive writing forms: interjoined, fluid, personal, and at times almost illegible. It is said, for example, that in extreme instances the calligraphy used to record poetry during the Heian and later eras would be virtually impossible to decipher unless its text were already known to the reader. Despite challenging legibility, the *sō* mode has produced works of exceptional beauty, whose aura transcends the linguistic message the writing was meant to convey. The paintings and calligraphy of Hon'ami Kōetsu (1558–1637) provide brilliant examples of this triumph of elegance over ease of comprehension. Between the *shin* and the *sō* forms is *gyō*, of the three modes the most vaguely defined, and thus the one most open to wide interpretation. In writing it perhaps connotes a mode more graceful than one rigidly *shin*, while still possessing an evident degree of clarity through which the meaning can be discerned. In terms of the garden, *gyō* might suggest a more or less rectangular stone whose single rough edge plays against its other three rigorously straight sides.

Over time these ideas, even when not consciously applied, influenced practically all Japanese spatial design, from the overall planning of temple complexes to the placement of a single stone. Even today, it serves as the basis of garden design and several schools of flower arrangement (*ikebana*). Applied to the garden, the mix of orders has given us walkways formal in overall aspect although composed of stones left in their natural state or reshaped only to a small degree. The key point is that the formal, semi-formal, and informal were not assigned to independent zones, but were embedded one within the other.

While the miniaturization characteristic of *bonsai*, or miniature trees, represents aesthetic pruning at its most extreme, at full scale shrubs are also clipped into singular forms (a technique called *karikomi* in Japanese)—which equates in large degree with the Western notion of topiary. [37, 38, 39]. What

35
CHÁ GORREANA TEA PLANTATION. AZORES, PORTUGAL.
THE ORIGINS OF ORNAMENTAL PRUNING PROBABLY DERIVE FROM FUNCTIONAL PRACTICES FIRST USED TO INCREASE PRODUCTION.

36
SHODEN-JI, KYOTO, JAPAN, 17TH CENTURY.
SHRUBS STAND IN FOR THE ROCKS MORE COMMON TO THE DRY GARDEN.

is the fascination—or to some, horror—generated by this "unnatural" treatment of shrubbery? Why should one natural material be reconfigured to appear as another, its natural growth constrained and guided into some new and curious shape? Perhaps one reason for our fascination and wonder—and at times questioning—stems from the tension between the natural form sought by the living plant and the control and reformation enacted by the gardener's shears. Pruning halts the flow of time and creates an eternal present uncharacteristic of living things. Whether geometric, as is more common in Japan; or animal or other whimsical forms, as in the West; pruning nevertheless hampers the pursuit of a genetic goal. If sufficiently subdued and submissive, the shrub metamorphoses into a green and living sculpture. Here perhaps we again confront the issues raised by the Linnean classification system that divides the kingdoms of living things into animal and vegetal. In an almost alchemical transformation: Voilà! Through poodling the vegetal can be rendered animal—well, at least in appearance.

## Tama-zukuri

The foliage of trees in Japanese gardens, as we have seen, has habitually been thinned to achieve a greater transparency and lighter mass. While shrubs were routinely reshaped, only rarely were the resulting forms figurative; more often shrubs were given geometric shapes such as cubes and bars that became foils for the organic forms of rocks or other shrubs that although pruned, nonetheless appear natural—at least to some degree.[21] The seventeenth-century hillside garden of Joju-in, a sub-temple of Kiyomizu-dera in southeastern Kyoto, derives much of its beauty and intrigue from a superb interplay of varied vegetal shapes, unusual rock forms, and a reflective pond—all topped off by a rather spectacular employ of borrowed scenery that captures the distant hills and enfolds it within the garden [40]. While combined into a magnificent composition, the vegetal elements have been treated individually—some geometrically. Arguably, nothing of the garden is truly "natural," except the rocks themselves.

Of all Japan's clipped shrubbery none rivals the great vegetal bulk that dominates the east garden at Daichi-ji in Shiga Prefecture, another product of the Edo Period (1603–1867) [41]. Here tight plantings of azaleas have merged over the years into a single volume of massive proportions; shearing has transformed the forms of the individual shrubs into a softly flowing landlocked wave. Disturbing the flow of this undulating volume are the cubic forms cut within its body to enact another play of *shin-gyō-sō*. Here the identity of any individual shrub bows to the collective form. In contrast to the quest for a unified form, poodling considers and sculpts all branches individually. Even when the planting extends linearly as a wall, each branch retains its identity and underscores the contribution of the part to the whole. Poodling thus respects the growth pattern of the plant—within limits, of course—as the gardener assiduously assesses the potential treatment of each branch and then acts accordingly.

At some point in time, the reduction of tree canopy density by selectively thinning needle and leaf clusters seems to have led to a greater consideration of the branch rather than the shrub as a totality. The foliage growing on the branch was now shaped individually, and could be clipped into spheres or umbrellas, or even given freer reign and allowed to extend along its branch [42]. This manner became known as the *tama-zukuri*—the sphere or ball style—whose practice appeared in the early years of the seventeenth century, perhaps even earlier.

The *tama-zukuri* is normally associated with gardens in the shogun's seat in Edo, today Tokyo, rather than with the emperor's court in Kyoto. To traditional Kyoto gardeners, in fact, the sphere style seems to have been disparaged as more than a bit vulgar and gauche. It is impossible to say whether this is an accurate recounting or merely legend and hearsay, however. But if true, this reaction to the new manner by traditional gardeners in Kansai strengthens the belief that the *tama-zukuri* did originate in Edo.

Restrictions against the entry of foreign ships into Japan began in the early years of the seventeenth century and remained in effect until the second half of the 1800s, when a number of trading ports were established by treaties coerced by the Western powers. During those years shortly after the opening of the country, the influx of Europeans and Americans, whether for business, political, or cultural purposes, brought new visitors to the gardens in and around the now-renamed capital of Tokyo. Given the Victorian predilection for the alpine rock garden and other vagaries of the Gardenesque style, English visitors were titillated, if often mystified, by what they encountered. Perhaps

37
JIKO-IN.
NARA, JAPAN,
17TH CENTURY.
UMBRELLA PRUNING.

38
REIUN-IN, TOKUFI-JI.
KYOTO, JAPAN.
16TH; 20TH CENTURIES.
RUGBY BALL PRUNING.

39
APARTMENT COURTYARD.
MASUDA, JAPAN.
GUMDROP PRUNING.

40 *(following page)*
KOBORI ENSHU.
JOJU-IN.
KYOTO, JAPAN,
EARLY 17TH CENTURY.
THE PLAY OF FORMALITIES
ENRICHES THE GARDEN'S
COMPOSITION

among those garden features that appeared the most peculiar were trees and shrubs with little balls of green at the ends of their branches. Most Victorian reactions to Japanese garden culture, and to its arts more broadly, were expressed simply as "curious," the exception being the high regard for the woodblock prints that had long been exported to the West, and which had exerted such a strong influence on European painting and printmaking.

In his impressively comprehensive study *Japanese Homes and Their Surroundings*, first published in 1888, New England scientist Edward S. Morse included a discussion of both gardens and the cultivation of miniature trees. Speaking of one visit, Morse wrote of a tree in "a large garden in Tokio that spread out in a symmetrical convex disk with a diameter of twenty feet or more, yet standing not over two feet in height." More closely related to poodling, a subject to which we shall return later in this essay, was another tree "in which the branches had been trained to assume the appearance of flattened disks" [43].[22] The practice becomes more intense, Morse notes, when *bonsai* plants are cultivated and raised under complete control, retarding and directing growth from the germination of their seeds. The illustrations in *Japanese Homes and Their Surroundings* include a branch form that suggests both the *tama-zukuri* manner of pruning as well as the "pizza" variety of poodling [see 76, 77]. Morse's observations and images also verify that Japanese pruning practices were applied to all sizes of plants from the miniature to the full-size, and that they could be found in temple gardens as well as those of private residences. These pruning techniques and their resultant aesthetic had percolated downward from the aristocracy to the general populace. Or had it been the other way around? Did *tama-zukuri* actually begin at the popular level, therefter appropriated, elevated, and transformed—as the tea masters had recast and sophisticated the rural farmhouse by applying the aesthetic of "refined poverty"? Regardless of the direction of the (horti)cultural flow, these examples clearly illustrate that the treatment of both the shrub as whole, and the branch as an element, had already achieved wide-spread acceptance in at least the country's two most important cities.

In 1877 Josiah Conder (1852–1920), a recently qualified British architect with limited office experience, arrived in Japan as the newly appointed Professor of Architecture at the Tokyo

Imperial College of Engineering, today a faculty of the University of Tokyo. Despite having been hired to teach Western building methods to aspiring Japanese architecture students, Conder was remarkably open to learning from the Japanese, unlike many of his ex-pat countrymen then living in the country. Like the Irishman Lafcadio Hearne, who transcribed folk tales and wrote essays and books to explain Japan to Western audiences, Conder sought to understand and then explain the making and meaning of the Japanese garden.[23] And he succeeded remarkably well. In *Landscape Gardening in Japan*, first published in 1893, Conder classified the gardens he had seen into several basic types, drawing from existing Japanese garden-making manuals for much of his content. In the book he described the treatment of the ornamental pine as a tree "pass[ing] through a sort of surgical treatment for the purpose of producing a shape of acknowledged beauty, as displayed in some of the finest natural trees of its species" [44]. More specifically, he wrote that, "Its branches are bent, broken, and bandaged with splints and cords, until they grow unassisted in the fancy shapes desired."[24] All to attain a "natural" effect, that has been achieved by, "clipping the short twigs and fasciculated leaves into the shape of a number of discs or flattened spheres." Here Conder notes that the manner is known as *tama-zukuri*.[25] Conder's book had an immediate and lasting impact—it remains in print even today—and in short order, the British and Americans were creating "Japanese gardens" abroad, on their estates or as commercial, social, or tourist venues. Rather than rigorously applying Conder's perceptive insights, these gardens were more often a pastiche using a standard mix of rocks, a small *torii*, some Japanese maples or cherry trees, and perhaps a miniature pagoda.[26] Those more adventurous might even have tried to shape their trees, which may have been the birth of poodling—especially in California where native Japanese gardeners or those of Japanese descent, were highly regarded in the making and maintaining of gardens. That trend was violently interrupted by the unlawful and tragic incarceration of Japanese-Americans and Japanese immigrants after the American entry into WW II.[27]

41 *(previous pages)*
DAICHI-JI.
SHIGA PREFECTURE, JAPAN.
17TH CENTURY.
TOPIARY AS GARDEN.

42
STACKED UMBRELLAS—
OR SHALLOW GUMDROPS?
TOKYO, JAPAN.

43 *(below left)*
"DWARFTED PINE."
[EDWARD MORSE,
*JAPANESE HOMES AND
THEIR SURROUNDINGS*]

44 *(below right)*
"PINE TREE."
[JOSIAH CONDER,
*LANDSCAPE GARDENING
IN JAPAN*]

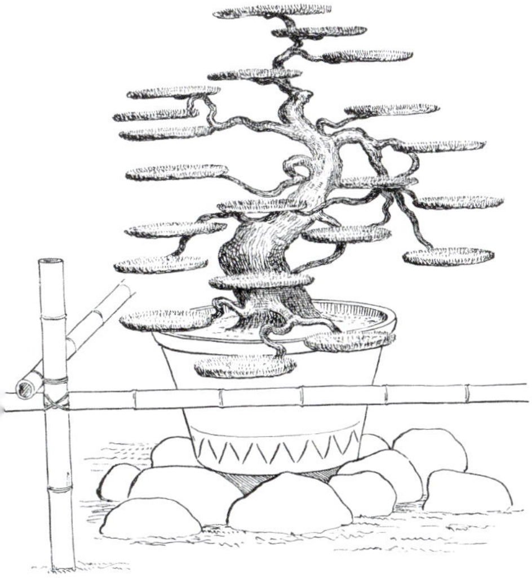

The conversion of *Canis lupus*, the wolf, to *Canis lupis familaris*, the domesticated dog, is believed to have taken place between 27,000 and 40,000 years ago, a process that elevated its status from wilderness threat to domestic asset. From the moment of the species' formation, until only a few centuries ago, the dog was regarded solely in terms of the work it could perform, especially for activities related to the hunt. Kept outdoors or housed in a barn or utility structure, the dog only very rarely set paw within the house. Over time, however, the relation between man's/woman's/their best friend became more endearing, and dogs began to be considered in a new light. In England, dogs still served the hunt, of course, but now in a more gentrified manner. Despite this change in use, they were usually kept as a pack and excluded from entry into the home or manor. That began to change in the seventeenth century, when in the mind of its owner the service animal metamorphosed from a utility to an object of affection. Formerly exiled to the kennel or farmyard, the dog was now accepted as a beloved member of the household [45]. In France during the eighteenth-century this transformation of regard became more widespread and the dog became, in Kathleen Kete's words, "the beast in the boudoir."[28]

Now "blessed" with a privileged interior life, the dog underwent further degrees of domestication, among them more extensive behavior training, deodorizing, and continued grooming. Madame's preference focused on small dogs, what today we might call lap dogs, who became a fashion accessory as well as fond friend. Accordingly, the breed and its breeding were continually brought up to date to reflect the current fashion. In time this care applied to the grooming of the animal as well, in particular the management of the dog's hair through shearing. Earlier on, dogs had been clipped for functional purposes: to retard the accumulation of mud and spurs or to reduce the external measure of the head or body part for increased speed while in pursuit, or to allow greater access into some burrow or tree hollow. As in horticulture in general, and the propagation of tea in particular, what had first emerged as a practice to address functional needs became a practice solely for display, cooing, and other aesthetic and social purposes. Shearing and clipping were used to manage the coats of a number of breeds, but over the years severe hair management became associated with a single breed: the poodle.

45
THE CLASSIC POODLE CLIP.
[DRAWING:
ALYSSA SCHWANN]

Despite our common association of the poodle with France, the breed actually had its origins in Germany, there known as the *püdel*, a hunting and water dog. The name "poodle" derives from this name, a shortening of *püdelhund*, which signified a "water dog." *Püdeln* in old German meant "splash," by the way, and shares the same root as the English word "puddle."[29] At one time, the coat of the dog's rear body was shorn to facilitate flotation and movement when swimming, while its mane and upper body were left uncut to retain warmth when the dog swam in cold water. It is said that the puffs of hair on its paws, or at the joints of its legs that we today read as ornamental, protected the dog "from cold and injury and...help[ed] prevent rheumatism."[30] Shearing allowed the lower body to move more freely in water, while clipping the long hair over the eyes, or tying it in a topknot, removed potential impediments to the dog's vision and mobility. "Owners eventually tied these knots with brightly colored ribbons to help them identify their dogs from afar."[31] Or so it is said by some.

Bred as a retriever, to enhance performance on the hunt the thick coat of the *püdel* was also selectively trimmed to reduce the weight gained when saturated with water. Early on, the legs were trimmed to grant the animal greater balance and freedom while swimming, and to aid in keeping the dog's head above water as it paddled.[32] Over time, however, more of the hair was selectively clipped, almost always to enhance the dog's performance on the hunt. Only later, when adopted as a domestic pet in France, was clipping reduced to a purely beautifying practice. In this transference from a functional procedure to an aesthetic predilection, the shaping of the poodle's fur closely parallels the transformation of the functional pruning of shrubs such as the tea plant to an ornamental garden form. What began in need metamorphosed into an amusement.

In her wonderful study of the domestication of the *Canus lupus domesticus*, Kete looks closely at the changes to regard and care that accompanied the transference of the dog's home base from barnyard to bedroom.[33] Not only were the breeds selectively reduced in size—hence the eventual arrival of the miniature or toy poodle—but also the basic attitude and purpose for which the animal was bred.

With domestication came new problems that required resolution: cleanliness, odor control, and obedience among them.[34] Living quasi-feral on the grounds of the estate, or in a barn or purpose-built shelter was one thing; being a presentable companion in the best of company and finest of homes was another. A smelly body, dirty paws, matted fur, and wayward demeanor would just not do. Over the years the solution to each of these hindrances to proper decorum was treated in publications that educated dog owners about the care needed to achieve the proper look and behavior. Among the upper classes the small dog became a fashion accessory: deodorized, glamorized, and fawned over almost as if a child—perhaps even more than the family's children. In France dog grooming and its groomers extend back to pre-revolutionary times.[35] In some instances the coat of the dog was even dyed colors, or the poor animal was dressed in an outfit and taught to do tricks.[36] Its foodways also changed. As an instrument for hunting the dog basically ate what the people ate, living on scraps of meat and other discards from the table. Over the years however, the dog's diet became more specifically adjusted to the animal, to satisfy its love of meat and inherent being as an omnivore. In response to this perceived need, an industry arose that specialized in the "proper" food for the dog—oh yes, and also for the cat.

Kete stresses the infantilism that accompanied the dog's entry into polite company, perhaps even as a surrogate for the child missing from the home, or as a more acceptable and trainable creature than some willful boy or girl. "Like children, pets needed to be trained, gently but firmly," writes Kate.[37] In addition, the body of the dog, or at least its coat, was treated as almost a sculptural material:

> *Canine coiffure also ingeniously removed beastly characteristics from animals in the home. Canine fur was shaped to resemble clothing, most obviously in hairstyles for poodles: the "lion cut," the "'English cut,'" and the coil shape* (tonte en macarons)*, to name three of the most common fin de siècle cuts.*[38]

Perhaps the lion cut was just a fashion, perhaps it was in emulation of the king of beasts, thereafter enacted at a far smaller scale on a beast of far different strength and demeanor. It could be said, however, that the clipped dog was as much a display of groomer prowess as it was about the appearance of our furry friend, which may remain true even today.

As these styles of dog grooming became popular and widespread long before the arrival of electric clippers, blow dryers, and hair conditioners, scissors, comb, and brush served as the principal tools for grooming both corded and curly hair. Over time the *barbet*, a larger, thick-coated dog used for hunting water fowl, was displaced by the smaller and more manageable *petit barbet* as the most fashionable breed. To be suitable for carriage in the arms of its mistress on her outings to the Bois de Boulogne or other popular venue, the dog's grooming was required to be pristine and impeccable.[39] It was "well combed, freshly clipped, its legs ornamented with bracelets of fur, a pompom at the tip of its tail, wearing a handsome collar set off by silver bells."[40] As the years passed the *petit barbet* became the most popular breed in pre-Revolutionary France and the breed most likely to seen in its salons and on fashionable promenades.

Although, as we have seen, clipped fur forms had their origins in function, it is not difficult to find comparisons in the garb and hairstyles worn in the royal courts of seventeenth- and eighteenth-century France. Take the Sun King, Louis XIV for example. As seen in grand portraits, such as the celebrated painting by Hyacinthe Rigaud, Louis displays a "well-turned" leg clad in tights emerging from his fur-trimmed regal robes [46]. Heels of a noticeable height add to his stature and dignity. Upon his head is a formidable wig—or is it really his own hair?—parted in the center and flowing downward on either side in a veritable cascade of ripples. We might also note that the wigs still worn by English judges at trial reflect a related form. When seen in this light, the hairstyles given poodles do not appear so different from their human contemporaries [47]. For one, the head in some poodle cuts—such as variants of the Continental—clip the mane in a not dissimilar manner. Although the legs are shaved back, the tufted hair on the feet is allowed to grow out or treated as a ball at the end of a stick—not unlike the fashion for having the lacy cuff of a blouse emerge and flair from the shorter sleeves of a jacket. Is it not easy to discern similar predilections in the treatment of these features and the link between human dress and the grooming of poodles? And from these parallels between human and canine, can we not extend the analogy to the branches of shrubs treated in a similar manner, i.e., those that have been poodled?

In the *Poodle Clipping Book,* Miss Cameo, nom de plume of one Mrs. Kay Waldschmidt, illustrates the hair styles she deems appropriate for today's—or at least the 1960s—poodle.[41] The two classic types—those required for show by the American Kennel Club are the Continental, which shears the better part of the poodle's rear half; and the English Saddle, which maintains more of the hair though modeling it into masses and muffs [48, 49]. The book's illustrations include "over 50" variants of poodle clipping, some displaying extremes of form that border on the those whose fantasy has guided the poodling of shrubs. Take for example the Banded Bolero Dutch, a cut that shapes a clump of fur on the top of the head into a canine beret, and a snug sweater-like mass around the forepaws and chest and hindquarters; all of this is topped off with pompoms at the bottom of each paw, and like the cherry on a sundae, a perfect ball of hair that survives at the end of the tail [50]. The Town and Country, in turn, takes a far different tact, shearing and softly shaping a coat of hair left almost intact, excepting most of the snoot—although not its very end—and the almost requisite puff at the end of the tail [51]. Between those two extremes are a host of styles that vary considerably in their play of massed hair against exposed skin, and in their degree of caprice and artistic invention. Needless to say, after the advent of the electric clippers, sculpting hair and fur became far less challenging tasks than in the past, when scissors and shears served as the primary instruments.

In many, if not most poodle cuts, the principal features of the clip are found in puffs at the ends of the dog's extremities. So too the foliage at the end of the branch after poodling. What worked well for Louis XIV's garb at Versailles enjoyed equal success when transplanted into the unprepossessing territory of the everyday garden.

46 *(following pages)*
HYACINTHE RIGAUD.
*PORTRAIT OF LOUIS XIV (detail)*, 1701.
[LOUVRE; WIKICOMMONS]

47
POODLE ROYALE.
[SHUTTERSTOCK]

48. 49
CLASSIC POODLE CUTS:
THE CONTINENTAL.
THE ENGLISH SADDLE.
[ALYSSA SCHWANN,
DRAWINGS AFTER
MISS CAMEO, *POODLE
CLIPPING BOOK*]

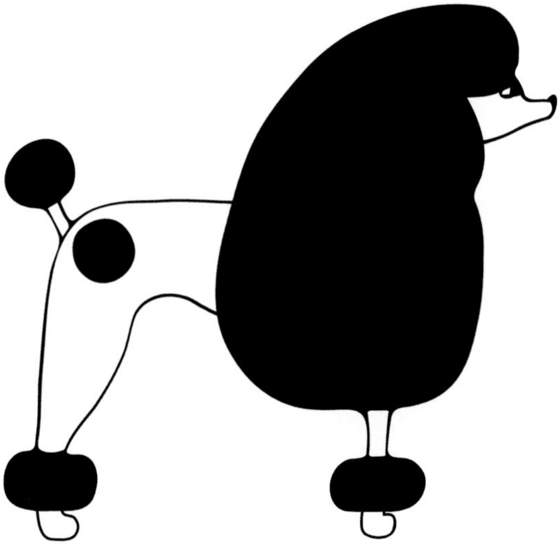

50, 51
CLASSIC POODLE CUTS:
THE BOLERO DUTCH.
THE TOWN AND COUNTRY.
[ALYSSA SCHWANN,
DRAWINGS AFTER
MISS CAMEO, *POODLE CLIPPING BOOK*]

*Although we may dismiss the binomialism and division of the vegetal and animal worlds demanded by Linnean taxonomy, we nonetheless must acknowledge differences is poodling practices. All poodling is not created equal. Some poodling is spread out, each branch culminating in small shaped vegetation, while according to other* schools, *leaf or needle masses remain so dense that they appear ingrown and hardly qualify as poodling as commonly understood [52, 53, 54, 55].* At this point the distinction between poodling and topiary blurs. Of course, it could be claimed that all shaped vegetation falls under the greater umbrella of topiary. Agreed. But it seems to me that when pruning takes a different turn, and the gardener or *topiarius* treats the shrub branch-by-branch rather than as a whole, we are dealing with a different animal—uh, plant. In the examples pictured in this book, we can establish certain differences between topiary and poodling, and identify some—but certainly not all—of the various forms that poodling has assumed. Clipping the branches, leaves, and needles of trees and shrubbery into layers—as previously noted, a common practice in Japan—occupies an intermediate category. While the overall shape of the tree or shrub may prevail, each branch is coerced into a horizontal green platter, and exists in an intermediate state between topiary and poodling.

The dense or ingrown forms noted above occupy the shifting border between the two realms of pruning. The garden of the Filoli estate, on the San Francisco peninsula in Woodside, California, contains a plethora of these densely poodled forms [56, 57]. Whether they were intended by Bruce Porter, the garden's original designer, is not known, but I would venture that they were not, and that they have evolved into their present forms in the continued negotiations between shrub and gardener. Their densely packed volumes could also be read as an expression of the gardener's inability to coax the shrub into a single topiaried event. Instead, each tree has declared its independence from the gardener's intentions and over time has dictated its own mature form. As a result, although very densely packed, each branch has been clipped into a distinct volume, that at times is maintained in near adjacency, at other times pruned to allow light and air to infiltrate the green masses clumped on the branches. Some branches remain staunchly sovereign and maintain their positions, while others have

52
PIN CUSHION POODLING,
(SUBSPECIES: SPARCE).
BERKELEY, CALIFORNIA.

53
PIN CUSHION,
OR BALL FORMS.
EL CERRITO, CALIFORNIA.

54
VEGETAL RUGBY BALLS.
EL CERRITO, CALIFORNIA.

55
CLUSTERED BALLS.
EL CERRITO, CALIFORNIA.

56
HYBRID POODLED FORMS.
FILOLI ESTATE, WOODSIDE,
CALIFORNIA.
IT EVEN *LOOKS* LIKE A
POODLE!

*(following pages)*
57
BALLS AND
RUGBY BALLS.
FILOLI ESTATE, WOODSIDE,
CALIFORNIA

58
POODLED WALL.
KYOTO, JAPAN.

59
POODLED SHRUBS
AS BOUNDARY WALL.
BERTHÅGA CEMETERY,
UPPSALA, SWEDEN.

60
POODLED PINE WALL
WITH BIRCHES EMERGING.
BERTHÅGA CEMETERY,
UPPSALA, SWEDEN.

61
A RUNWAY OF POODLED
JUNIPERS LONGING
TO BE FREE.
BERKELEY, CALIFORNIA.

bowed under the weight of the vegetation they have been forced to bear. At this stage vegetation may come to resemble animal forms, although that was probably not the designer's intention. If extended laterally, a conglomerate of poodled shrubs may take form as a poodled wall, or if extended horizontally, as a carpet [58, 59, 60, 61]. Although clipped independently, most often the masses of the branches of these agglomerations visually merge into one another, with their final visage transformed into a highly tufted rug set vertically that can extend for hundreds of feet.

If clusters of ingrown greenery suggest one connection between poodling and topiary, the true missing link between them might be found in Tule, Oaxaca, Mexico, nearby the celebrated *ahuehuete* (Montezuma bald cypress, *Taxodium mucronatum*), which is believed to have the world's stoutest trunk. However, that magnificent tree serves only to lead us to the small lawn enclosed by rows of shrubs that carpets the garden fronting the church of Santa María del Tule. There, a number of the garden's small shrubs have been graced with distinctly cut figures [62, 63, 64]. Not the entire shrub, mind you: the individual branches have been treated as topiary, in contrast to the simple masses characteristic of standard poodling. Each branch thus becomes a topiary in miniature, figurative and neatly clipped. Pruning branch-by-branch marks this as poodling; the figures at each branch end instead suggest topiary. So what are they? Or should we enter these shrubs in a genus of its own? Perhaps fabulous works like these might comprise a new type we might reluctantly call "topiapoodling."

We feel obliged to caution the reader about the existence of a bastard form best termed "faux-poodling," that results from natural growth rather than the human hand. The practice of pollarding species such as London plane trees (*Platanus acerfolia*) is international, the annual removal of the year's growth of branches and leaves that results in a more compact tree form marked by stubby knobs at the ends of the major branches. This operation encourages the growth of a dense tree canopy, but also maintains the health and longevity of the tree—or so it is said. In years past, the cuttings derived from pollarding were given practical uses like the making of fences or used as firewood by those in need: a sort of arboreal harvesting for the hearth. In the springtime, as the tree responds to improving weather conditions and warmer temperatures, it begins to sprout leaves [65]. These can appear anywhere along the branch, but most often these leaf concentrations begin at the ends of their amputated limbs. At first glance these clusters may appear as a poodled effort, but do not be fooled! These sprouts are not the product of a gardener's efforts, but must be dismissed as simply a green springtime mirage.

The list of categories below, while neither exclusive nor exhaustive, attempts to cover the primary shapes discovered during my continuing hunt for representative examples of poodling. These include the more or less spherical Pincushion or Ball, whose Marshmallow variants result from a rounding of their edges [66, 67, 68]; the attenuated mass that extends linearly along the branch is appropriately termed the Pickle, or alternatively known as the Microphone [69]. The Cube is marked by strict cuts and strong geometric definition; if given rounded edges the effect is softened; with the Pincushion, it shares a Marshmallow or Gumdrop variant [70]. The extended length and rounded form of another pruned shape suggests Rugby Ball as an appropriate name, with its extreme elongation assigned to the subcategory of Caterpillar [71, 72, 73]. Given its gently rounded upper profile, the Umbrella appears capable of shedding water, while delighting us with the play between its curved upper surface and flat bottom. A mass round in plan, yet shallow in depth, warrants the moniker Pizza, especially when these are stacked in layers, as if ready for take-out. Thickened in depth, the Pizza is cataloged as the Deep Dish variant [76, 77].

Of course, this list of basic categories is incomplete and at best imprecise. Every gardener creates her/his/their own versions based on the shrub in question and the conditions under which it grows. The basic types identified here are often augmented and enhanced by using varying forms of clipping, even within a single shrub [78, 79, 80, 81]. No rules or ruling bodies govern the practice of poodling. Its forms are limited only by the gardener's available time, tools, skill, and creativity.

62, 63, 64
TOPIAPOODLING.
THULE, MEXICO.
THE MISSING LINK
BETWEEN TOPIARY
AND POODLING,
WITH EACH BRANCH
INDIVIDUALLY PRUNED
INTO A FIGURE.

65
FAUX-POODLING:
POLLARDED STREET TREES.
TURKU, FINLAND.

Who poodles? Over the years, I have caught very few poodlers in the act. Of the half dozen of so I have had the privilege to meet, and those with whom I've talked, all were retired folk with relatively small gardens, some few shrubs, and a lot of time on their hands. That said, most of the poodlers told me that their shrubs required pruning only twice a year. Junipers were the mostly commonly used species; others may demand more frequent attention. Of course, not all the gardens pictured in this book are maintained by the owners. Those in parks, commercial zones, and even some private houses are often cared for by professional gardeners or gardening services. Just who decides how to answer the question "To poodle or not to poodle?" is not known, but one would imagine that the owner of the property must be committed to maintaining the shrubs in their clipped state. If not, the shrub soon forgets the initial trim and over time grows to assume the form for which it was genetically programmed. Continued effort is required. When left to their own dreams and devices, the top surfaces of the plants will grow and send up growth that might be termed "poodling flambé." This growth is particularly characteristic of juniper [see 75]. Should you look carefully, you'll discover that a number of the shrubs included in this book have already begun to recover their natural forms by sending shoots vertically in search of sunlight.

In baseball, with its game of nine innings, the visiting team bats first. We could say that the gardener working in nature represents the visitors; nature and natural processes represent the home team. Throughout the game the gardener may seem to be winning, with the growth of the shrubs controlled and guided by shearing into the various desired forms. But bear in mind that if nature is the home team, it is nature that bats last. As a result, poodling is hardly eternal. Some may rejoice; others will mourn.

Note: *To the best of my knowledge, the term* poodling *was coined by Bay Area landscape architect and educator Chris Grampp in an article published perhaps in* Landscape *magazine, perhaps as long ago as the 1980s. Unfortunately I have been unable to locate that particular article, but I do wish to give credit where credit is due.*

1 In *Second Nature: A Gardener's Education*, Michael Pollan discusses how peer pressure shapes the maintenance of the suburban residential landscape, and that a lack of care for one's front lawn can be interpreted as antisocial behavior and a disrespect for one's neighbors. (New York: Dell, 1991), p. 23.

2 Miles Hadfield, *Topiary and Ornamental Hedges: Their History and Cultivation* (London: Adam & Charles Black, 1971), p. 13.

3 Centre national de ressources textuelles et lexicales, https://www.cnrtl.fr/definition/espalier

4 École superieure du Paysage at Versailles was established in 1996, although its horticultural roots extend back to 1874.

5 See Anatole Tchikine, "Boxwood: A Plant That Took Over the Garden World." Dumbarton Oaks, Plant Humanities, 2021. https://lab.plant-humanities.org/boxwood/

6 Postcard in author's collection.

7 Joseph Addison, *The Spectator*, No. 414, 25 June 1712; reprinted in John Dixon Hunt and Peter Willis, eds., T*he Genius of the Place: The English Landscape Garden 1620–1820* (Cambridge MA: MIT Press, 1988), pp. 142–43.

8 Alexander Pope, *Epistle to Lord Burlington*, 1731; reprinted in Hunt and Willis, *Genius of the Place*, p. 213.

9 Anonymous, *The Rise and Progress of the Present Taste in Plantin*g, 1767; John Harris, ed., facsimile edition (Newcastle upon Tyne: Oriel Press, 1970), p. 8.

10 Addison, *The Spectato*r, No. 414; reprinted in Hunt and Willis, *Genius of the Place*, p. 143.

11 Mark Twain, *Innocents Abroad, or New Pilgrim's Progress*, 1869; (reprint New York: Modern Library, 2003), p. 106.

12 Twain, *Innocents Abroad*, pp. 107, 108.

13 Twain, *Innocents Abroad*, p. 108.

14 Twain, *Innocents Abroad*, p. 108.

15 William Robinson, *The Wild Garden*, 1870 (Project Gutenberg eBook, 2014), p. 112.

16 Ironically, Robinson's own garden at Gravetye Manor (1911) was laid out on a series of grassed terraces, with the planting arranged around the perimeter and in the adjacent woodland. He seemed to sense the need for providing some sort of formal structure for all the informal plantings. Richard Bisgrove, *William Robinson: The Wild Gardener* (London: Frances Lincoln, 2008).

17 In 2008, when I last visited Levens Hall, the boxwood were threatened by the spread of a blight. Hopefully they have survived and its wonderful topiary recreated using a more resistant strain of boxwood.

18 "Welcome to Green Animals Topiary Garden," brochure (Newport: Preservation Society of Newport County, 2018).

19 J.C. Loudon, sources not listed, quoted in Hadfield, *Topiary and Ornamental Hedges*, p. 48

20 Of course, today this has reached an extreme in genetic modification; many of the same arguments used against GMO products were those used against topiary and poodling.

21 "In certain gardens trees or shrubs are trained and trimmed into forms intended to imitate a ship or junk in full sail, even a lantern or a shrine may be represented in such greenery; but these exceptional examples possess the merit of portraying objects not out of place in natural scenery." Josiah Conder, *Landscape Gardening in Japan* (Tokyo: Hakubunsha, 1893), p. 109.

22 Edward S. Morse, *Japanese Homes and Their Surroundings*, 1886 (reprint, New York Dover, 1961), p. 288.

23 Lafcadio Hearne, *A Japanese Miscellany: Strange Stories; Folklore Gleanings; Studies Here & There,* 1901 (reprint, Rutland VT: Charles E. Tuttle, 1954); *Gleanings in Buddha-Fields: Studies of Hand and Soul in the Far East*, 1897 (reprint, Rutland VT: Charles E. Tuttle, 1971); *Exotics and Retrospectives*, 1898 (reprint, Rutland VT: Charles E. Tuttle, 1971).

24 Conder, *Landscape Gardening in Japan*, p. 108.

25 Conder, *Landscape Gardening in Japan*, p. 109.

26 See Kendall Brown, *Japanese-Style Gardens of the Pacific West Coast* (New York: Rizzoli, 1999).

27 Many of the first generation of landscape architects working in California were the children of immigrant or first-generation farmers or gardeners.

28 Kathleen Kete, *The Beast in the Boudoir: Petkeeping in Nineteenth-century Paris* (Berkeley: University of California, 1994). I have relied heavily on this book in the following discussion.

29 Interestingly, the word *poodle* is not used by the French, who prefer the *barbet* and the *caniche*, the former larger like today's standard poodle, the second, the smaller or miniature breed.

30 Jill Hunter Pellettieri, "Why Are Poodle Haircuts So Weird?" *Slate*, 10 February 2004. https://slate.com/news-and-politics/2004/02/the-genesis-of-the-poodle-hairdo.html

31 Pellettieri, "Why Are Poodle Haircuts So Weird?"

32 Mary E. Thurston, "Dog grooming through the ages," *DogWorld*, April 1993, p. 15.

33 Kete, *The Beast in Boudoir*, p. 78.

34 Kete quotes Jean Robert that the task was "'to make the dog into as agreeable a companion as possible,'" a matter of "deanimalization, feminization, and control." *Le chien d'appartement et d'utilité: Education, dressage, hygène, maladies*, Paris: 1888, p. 97), quoted in *The Beast in Boudoir*, p. 79.

35 Kete, *The Beast in Boudoir*, p. 88.

36 Kete, *The Beast in Boudoir*, p. 81.

37 Kete, *The Beast in Boudoir*, p. 82.

38 Paul Mégnin, *Nos chiens, Races, dressage, élevage, hygène, maladie*s, Paris: 1909, p. 327, quoted by Kete, p. 86.

39 Del Dahl, *The Complete Poodle Book* (New York: Howell Book House, p. 2).

40 Mme. Charles Boesvwillward, *Chien de luxe: Comment élever, dresser, et soigner nos chiens*, Paris 1907, p, 204, quoted by Kete, *The Beast in Boudoir*, p. 87.

41 Miss Cameo (Mrs. Kay Waldschmidt), *Poodling Clipping Book* (T.F.H. Publica tions, 1962).

SPEED
LIMIT
25

66 *(opposite)*
A GAGGLE OF CLASSIC
PINCUSHIONS.
SANTA ROSA, CALIFORNIA.

67
POODLED BALLS
AND BRANCHES.
BERKELEY, CALIFORNIA.

68
MARSHMALLOWS,
OR CUBES WITH
SOFTENED EDGES.
DAVIS, CALIFORNIA.

69
PICKLE OR MICROPHONE
POODLING.
BERKELEY, CALIFORNIA

70
A MARSHMALLOW JUNTA.
SCOTTSDALE, ARIZONA.

*(following pages)*
71
A CORNUCOPIA OF
RUGBY BALLS ON
A TRIAD OF TREES.
WATSONVILLE, CALIFORNIA.

72
POODLED UMBRELLA FORMS.
KAIRAKU-EN,
MITO, JAPAN.

73
A MELANGE OF
POODLED FORMS.
LE JARDIN JAPONAIS.
COURANCES, FRANCE,
20TH CENTURY.

74 *(opposite)*
A TIERED STACK
OF UMBRELLAS.
SHIMOSUWA, JAPAN.

75
CREEPING MASSES OF
ELOGATED RUGBY BALLS,
WITH TOUCHES OF FLAMBÉ
GROWTH.
ARCUEIL, FRANCE.

*(following pages)*
76
CLASSIC EXAMPLES
OF THE PIZZA CUT.
BERKELEY, CALIFORNIA.

77
A DENSE MASS O'
DEEP-DISH PIZZAS.
BERKELEY, CALIFORNIA.

1229

1300

78
A POTFUL OF INTIMATE PIN CUSHIONS.
KLEIN GLIENICKE, POTSDAM, GERMANY.

79 *(opposite)*
A POWERFUL CLUSTER OF MARSHMALLOWISH PIN CUSHIONS.
LAS VEGAS, NEVADA.

*(following pages)*
80
SPIKEY PINE RUGBY BALLS.
SANTA ROSA, CALIFORNIA.

81
A VERITABLE ZOO OF VARIED POODLED FORMS.
YUBA CITY, CALIFORNIA.

SUTTER

COUNTY

82

POODLING IN THE NORTH.
HARRISON HOT SPRINGS,
BRITISH COLUMBIA,
CANADA.
POODLING IS EVERYWHERE.